ÉRIC]

p

Journey to the
Heart of Pétanque

Its history, its types of play, its rules

The Art of Shooting, Pointing, and Winning!

Published by Pierre Semard Editions

"Pétanque is a game where the pleasure of playing is as important as the victory."

Éric Borowiak

Preface

Welcome to the captivating world of pétanque, a sport that combines competition, precision, and conviviality. Each chapter of this book is dedicated to a fundamental aspect of pétanque, from mastering shots to game strategy, including the secrets of precise pointing and memorable victories that define this discipline. You will also explore the essential equipment for pétanque players and the delicate art of maintaining your boules.

Pétanque has a fascinating history, originating in La Ciotat, Provence, at the beginning of the 20th century, thanks to the ingenuity of Mr. Jules Lenoir, a player afflicted with rheumatism whose story you will discover within these pages. Whether you are a beginner or an experienced player, this book will immerse you in this fabulous epic.

Discover the values and rules of pétanque, explore various game strategies such as the famous "You shoot or you point," and familiarize yourself with its unique vocabulary. At the end of the book, an explanatory glossary will clarify expressions such as "win the lead" or "play fanny."

Whether you aim for victory in tournaments, enjoyable moments with friends on the field, or simply a better understanding of the subtleties of pétanque, this comprehensive book will be your guide on your journey towards excellence in this traditional and exciting game. Prepare to dive into the world of pétanque, where precision and strategy are the keys to success, and where each game offers the opportunity to create unforgettable memories.

Acknowledgements

I wish to express my gratitude to everyone who shared their advice and knowledge, whether professional players or enlightened amateurs I have met throughout France. I also extend a special thank you to the professionals who traveled to the pétanque stadium in Yssingeaux to participate in the 2024 Bol d'Or Pétanque, a 24-hour non-stop pétanque competition, for their availability. This competition was organized by Zvonko Radnic, vice-world champion of pétanque, European champion, multiple French champion, and most recently French and European club champion with his Arlanc club in 2022.

I would like to extend my heartfelt thanks to the online news journal La Commère43, which plays a vital role in our community in Haute-Loire and neighboring departments by providing relevant local information on events, cultural activities, and news. Their support is invaluable and greatly contributes to the richness of our regions.

Éric Borowiak

TABLE OF CONTENTS

Pétanque,
A Whole History

Éric Borowiak, Journey to the Heart of Pétanque

Pétanque: A Whole History

Pétanque is a boules game that evolved from the traditional Provençal game, which had been played for centuries in the Provence region of France. The Provençal game involved throwing a wooden boule towards a small wooden ball, the cochonnet, with the goal of getting as close as possible to it while preventing the opponent from doing so.

The pétanque we know today was invented in La Ciotat, Provence, in the early 20th century. The story goes that a Provençal player named Jules Lenoir, suffering from rheumatism, could no longer perform the jumps and movements required in the traditional game. To continue playing despite his mobility issues, he decided to remain stationary and throw the boules from a fixed point, with his feet together. This new method was adopted by his friends, including Ernest Pitiot, who popularized this version of the game.

The term "pétanque" itself comes from the Provençal "pèd tanco," which literally means "feet together." Thus, the game of pétanque was born, with players throwing their boules from a fixed circle while remaining immobile.

Over time, pétanque became increasingly popular in France and around the world, and it is now a boules sport played by millions of people. It has become a symbol of conviviality and relaxation, often played in village squares.

La Ciotat, the Cradle of Pétanque

Éric Borowiak, Journey to the Heart of Pétanque

La Ciotat: The Cradle
of Pétanque

La Ciotat, the Love of Pétanque

La Ciotat, a charming coastal village in Provence, is more than just a Mediterranean haven. It is the birthplace of pétanque, a game that has captured the hearts and souls of the locals and beyond. The love story between La Ciotat and pétanque is rich in tradition, innovation, and conviviality.

The Birth of Pétanque

Pétanque, as we know it today, was born in 1910 in La Ciotat. Jules Lenoir, a resident suffering from rheumatism, could no longer play traditional boules games that required running. His friend, Ernest Pitiot, adapted a version of the game where players could remain stationary. They played "pieds tanqués" (feet planted), giving rise to the term "pétanque." This game, combining precision and strategy, quickly spread throughout the region.

Square Eugène Mouton: The Heart of Pétanque

The Jules Lenoir Association continues to honor pétanque on the very ground where the game was born. It organizes tournaments under the plane trees, recreating the atmosphere of the early 20th century. Recently, Square Eugène Mouton, dedicated to the former mayor of La Ciotat, has become a must-visit spot for pétanque enthusiasts. Whether during sunny days or warm summer evenings, this iconic place always attracts a crowd. Its warm and authentic atmosphere makes it a prime location for meetings and relaxation.

Pétanque and Filmmakers

La Ciotat is also famous for its connection to cinema. The Lumière brothers, pioneers of cinema, had a summer residence in La Ciotat, where they shot several of their early films. This connection between cinema and La Ciotat attracted many artists and filmmakers who discovered and adopted pétanque, contributing to its popularity.

Celebrities and Pétanque

Over the decades, La Ciotat has become a favored spot for French and international celebrities. Actors like Fernandel and Yves Montand, as well as sports figures like Zinedine Zidane, have often been seen playing pétanque. Their affection for the game has reinforced La Ciotat's image as the cradle of pétanque.

Pétanque Tournaments

La Ciotat hosts annual pétanque tournaments that draw players from all over France and beyond. The most famous tournament is the "Grand Prix de la Ville de La

Ciotat," which brings together the best players in a festive and competitive atmosphere. These events are highlights of local life, where passion for the game and community spirit come together.

Pétanque Today

Today, pétanque remains a central element of life in La Ciotat. Residents continue to gather for daily games, perpetuating a tradition that blends sport and conviviality. Pétanque is more than just a game; it is a way of life that reflects the soul of La Ciotat.

An Art of Living

In La Ciotat, pétanque is much more than a pastime. It embodies the Provençal spirit, where every game is an opportunity to celebrate friendship, community, and the joy of life. Whether playing or watching a game, everyone finds a moment of happiness and sharing.

La Marseillaise
à Pétanque

Éric Borowiak Voyage au cœur de la pétanque

The Marseillaise
à Pétanque

Marseille, Pétanque, and the Art of Living

The love story between Marseille and pétanque is a saga where tradition and fame meet, in a city where the game embodies the very soul of local culture. Marseille, with its iconic port and vibrant neighborhoods, is the cradle of pétanque, a game that has charmed generations of Marseillais and celebrities worldwide over the decades.

The Place of Pétanque in Marseille

In Marseille, every neighborhood has its own pétanque ground, known as a "boulodrome." The most famous of these is probably Parc Borély, where locals gather to play under the sun. Pétanque here is more than just a game; it is a true institution.

The 1950 and 1960: Marseille and Cinema

During the 1950s and 1960s, Marseille became a favored filming location for French cinema. Directors like Marcel Pagnol captured the essence of Marseillaise life, where pétanque often played a central role. Pagnol's films, with actors like Fernandel, cemented the image of Marseille and pétanque in the collective imagination.

Celebrities and Pétanque

Marseille also attracts international celebrities. Yves Montand, a local boy, often returned to his hometown to play pétanque with residents. Similarly, personalities like Jean-Paul Belmondo and Alain Delon were often seen playing pétanque during their visits to Marseille, helping to popularize the game far beyond Provence's borders.

The Marseillaise à Pétanque

The Marseillaise à pétanque is an iconic pétanque tournament, renowned for being one of the most prestigious in the world. Created in 1962 by the daily newspaper "La Marseillaise," this annual tournament takes place in Marseille, attracting thousands of participants and spectators.

The tournament is open to all, amateurs and professionals alike, with teams of three players, known as "triplettes." The competition progresses through several phases, starting with eliminations and moving through the main rounds, quarter-finals, semi-finals, and finally the grand finale. The rules followed are those defined by the International Federation of Pétanque and Provençal Game (FIPJP).

The Marseillaise à pétanque stands out for its international reach, welcoming teams from around the world, including many national and international champions. The event enjoys significant media coverage, with television broadcasts and reports in the print and digital press, contributing to its renown.

Beyond the sporting competition, the Marseillaise à pétanque is a true cultural and social festival. Matches are mainly held in iconic Marseille locations such as Parc Borély, offering a picturesque and friendly setting. The atmosphere is festive and warm, with numerous spectators coming to cheer on the players and enjoy the entertainment and food stalls.

The Marseillaise à pétanque embodies the spirit of pétanque and the conviviality of Marseille, making it an unmissable event for enthusiasts of the sport and those wishing to experience Provençal culture.

Saint-Tropez,
the Love of Stars

Éric Borowiak, Journey to the Heart of Pétanque

Saint-Tropez,

the Love of the Stars

Saint-Tropez, the Love of the Stars and Pétanque

The love affair between Saint-Tropez and pétanque takes on a special dimension when you add the fascination of the stars for this picturesque village and its iconic game. For decades, Saint-Tropez has attracted celebrities from all over the world, and pétanque, with its timeless charm, has become a key symbol.

The Beginning of the Romance

It all starts with the history of pétanque, which was born in La Ciotat in 1910. However, this game quickly found a warm home in Saint-Tropez, a village whose relaxed, sunny atmosphere made it the ideal place to play boules. The Place des Lices or Place Carnot, shaded by centuries-old plane trees, became the heart of this tradition.

The 1950 and 1960: The Arrival of the Stars

In the 1950 and 1960, Saint-Tropez was thrust into the limelight thanks to icons like Brigitte Bardot. This actress, a symbol of glamour and freedom, fell in love with this little paradise. She settled in her villa "La Madrague" and attracted with her a host of international celebrities.

Pétanque and the Celebrities

It was on the Place des Lices that stars mingled with locals for pétanque games. Brigitte Bardot, Roger Vadim, Jean-Paul Belmondo, and many others discovered the simple pleasure of this Provençal game. Photos of these icons playing pétanque went around the world, forever associating Saint-Tropez and this game with conviviality and charm.

A Tradition That Endures

Today, the stars' passion for Saint-Tropez has not waned. Every summer, modern celebrities like Leonardo DiCaprio, Rihanna, or Kate Moss continue to visit this iconic village. And pétanque remains a must-do activity, a bridge between generations and cultures.

Tournaments and Events

Pétanque tournaments organized in Saint-Tropez attract passionate players from all over. These events are often an opportunity for celebrities to show a more relaxed and accessible side, sharing the court with locals and visitors.

An Art of Living

Pétanque in Saint-Tropez is more than a game; it's an art of living. It embodies the Provençal douceur de vivre, where time seems to stop, and each game is a celebration of life, friendship, and conviviality.

In conclusion, the love story between Saint-Tropez and pétanque is inseparable from the affection that stars have for this village. Together, they create a unique blend of glamour and tradition, making Saint-Tropez a place where charm and authenticity meet.

Saint-Paul-de-Vence,
a Star Village

Éric Borowiak, Journey to the Heart of Pétanque

Saint-Paul-de-Vence,

the Star Village

Saint-Paul-de-Vence, Art and Pétanque

Perched on the French Riviera, Saint-Paul-de-Vence is known for its picturesque charm, cobblestone streets, and love for art. But at the heart of this artists' haven lies a passion for a Provençal game that brings generations together: pétanque. The love story between Saint-Paul-de-Vence and pétanque is a unique blend of tradition, culture, and conviviality.

Place De Gaulle: Heart of Pétanque

In Saint-Paul-de-Vence, Place De Gaulle, commonly known as "place du jeu de boules," is the heart of pétanque. This historic spot, surrounded by ramparts and centuries-old trees, is where locals gather to play, chat, and share moments of conviviality. Place Neuve symbolizes the community spirit that animates this village.

The Arrival of the Artists

Saint-Paul-de-Vence became a haven for artists in the early 20th century. Painters like Marc Chagall and Aimé Maeght were drawn to the village's beauty and light. Chagall, who spent the last years of his life here, especially enjoyed watching pétanque games from the sunny terraces.

Stars and Pétanque

The 1950s and 1960s saw the arrival of many celebrities in the village, drawn by its charm and artistic atmosphere. Yves Montand and Simone Signoret, famous residents of Saint-Paul-de-Vence, often participated in pétanque games on Place Neuve. Their presence and love for the game helped reinforce Saint-Paul-de-Vence's image as a place where art and pétanque meet.

Pétanque Tournaments

Saint-Paul-de-Vence regularly organizes pétanque tournaments, attracting passionate players from all over the region. These events are festive occasions where visitors can experience the hospitality and conviviality of the locals.

Pétanque Today

Today, pétanque remains a central part of life in Saint-Paul-de-Vence. Locals and visitors continue to gather on Place Neuve for lively games, perpetuating a tradition that blends sport, relaxation, and conviviality.

An Art of Living

In Saint-Paul-de-Vence, pétanque is more than a pastime ; it embodies the Provençal art of living, where each game is an opportunity to celebrate friendship, community, and the simple beauty of life.

Chomérac Leads
"the Mène"

Éric Borowiak, Journey to the Heart of Pétanque

Chomérac Leads

the "Mène"

Chomérac: Shooting or Pointing?

Rooted in a rich history since Roman times, the picturesque town of Chomérac in Ardèche is preparing for an equally glorious future.

The French Pétanque Federation, seeking a new location for its headquarters, has set its sights on this charming town. A meticulous selection process among forty candidates culminated in Chomérac's victory, even outshining the Drôme prefecture, Valence.

Soon, Chomérac will become the nerve center of pétanque, hosting both the French and International Pétanque Federations. An ambitious project is underway, including the construction of 64 pétanque courts, a renowned training center, an official shop, and many other facilities on a spacious site just steps from the town center.

But Chomérac is not just a sports venue. Its eventful past since contemporary times, with its 19th-century milling activities and flourishing agricultural industry, testifies to its economic vitality. Today, with over 140 businesses, the town is thriving.

Social and cultural life is equally vibrant, punctuated by events throughout the year that showcase local traditions, craftsmanship, and Ardèche gastronomy. The residents, proud of their town, actively participate in this hustle and bustle, offering visitors an authentic and warm experience.

Rules and Regulations for Playing Pétanque

Playing pétanque follows relatively simple rules, although more formal competitions involve specific regulations. Here's an overview of the basic rules to better understand the game:

Team Composition

Pétanque is usually played in teams of two or three players. Each member has three pétanque balls.

Coin Toss

Before the game begins, a coin toss can be done to determine which team will start.

The Target or Cochonnet

A player from the team throws the target, also called the "cochonnet," to a specified distance on the field. The cochonnet must be positioned between 6 and 10 meters from the throwing circle.

Throwing the Balls

Players take turns throwing their balls to get as close as possible to the cochonnet. Throws must be made from a throwing circle, usually marked on the field.

Scoring Points

After all balls have been thrown, the team with the ball closest to the cochonnet scores points. Each ball closer to the cochonnet than any opposing ball counts as one point. The team retains control until the opponent places a ball closer to the cochonnet.

End of the Game

The game typically continues until a team reaches a predetermined number of points, often set at 13, 15, or 21 points, depending on the competition's rules or players' preferences. The team that reaches this score first wins the game.

Fouls

Fouls include stepping out of the throwing circle or incorrect ball throws. In case of a foul, the opponent can choose to leave the thrown balls as they are or place them according to the rules.

These basic rules may vary slightly by region or competition. It's recommended to consult specific regulations if you participate in official competitions. By following these rules, you can fully enjoy the pétanque experience.

Rules and Regulations
for Pétanque

Éric Borowiak, Journey to the Heart of Pétanque

Rules and Regulations

for Playing Pétanque

Playing pétanque follows relatively simple rules, although more formal competitions involve specific regulations. Here's an overview of the basic rules to better understand the game:

Team Composition

Pétanque is usually played in teams of two or three players. Each member has three pétanque balls.

Coin Toss

Before the game begins, a coin toss can be done to determine which team will start.

The Target or Cochonnet

A player from the team throws the target, also called the "cochonnet," to a specified distance on the field. The cochonnet must be positioned between 6 and 10 meters from the throwing circle.

Throwing the Balls

Players take turns throwing their balls to get as close as possible to the cochonnet. Throws must be made from a throwing circle, usually marked on the field.

Scoring Points

After all balls have been thrown, the team with the ball closest to the cochonnet scores points. Each ball closer to the cochonnet than any opposing ball counts as one point. The team retains control until the opponent places a ball closer to the cochonnet.

End of the Game

The game typically continues until a team reaches a predetermined number of points, often set at 13, 15, or 21 points, depending on the competition's rules or players' preferences. The team that reaches this score first wins the game.

Fouls

Fouls include stepping out of the throwing circle or incorrect ball throws. In case of a foul, the opponent can choose to leave the thrown balls as they are or place them according to the rules.

These basic rules may vary slightly by region or competition. It's recommended to consult specific regulations if you participate in official competitions. By following these rules, you can fully enjoy the pétanque experience.

Official Terrain Dimensions for Playing Pétanque

Éric Borowiak, Journey to the Heart of Pétanque

The Official Dimensions

of Pétanque Courts

There are official dimensions for the playing field that vary depending on the type of game and the level of competition. Here are the main specifications for a pétanque court:

Length and Width

For a classic pétanque game, the length of the court (distance between the throwing circles) should be at least 15 meters, though shorter courts may be used for casual play. The width should be about 4 meters.

Throwing Circles

At the beginning of each round (mène), a throwing circle is drawn on the ground. The circle should have a diameter of 50 centimeters and be traced 1 to 2 meters behind the throwing line. The player's feet must be entirely inside the circle when throwing the boule from this spot.

Space Between Courts

If several pétanque courts are side by side, there should be a separation of at least 1 meter between each court to avoid interference between ongoing games.

Marking the Court

The boundaries of the playing field should be clearly defined, for example, using plastic bands, strings, or lines drawn on the ground.

These dimensions are generally respected in official pétanque competitions, but for informal games, players may adapt the dimensions based on their available space and preferences. It's recommended to check the specific rules of the tournament or competition you participate in to ensure compliance with official rules.

Rules for Provençal Pétanque, Provençal Boules, and Lyonnaise Boules

Éric Borowiak, Journey to the Heart of Pétanque

Rules of Provençal Pétanque,

Provençal Boule,

and Lyonnaise Boule

Provençal Pétanque

Provençal Pétanque, also known as "jeu provençal" or "longue," follows these main rules:

Teams:

The game is played in teams of two, three, or four players.

Objective:

The game starts with the throw of the target ball, called the "but" or "bouchon." The target must be thrown at a distance between 15 meters and 20 meters from the throwing circle.

Throwing Circle:

As in standard pétanque, a throwing circle is marked on the ground. The player must have at least one foot inside the circle when throwing.

Throwing the Balls:

Each team has pétanque balls which they throw towards the target. The balls are thrown from behind the throwing circle.

Scoring:

The goal is to place your balls as close as possible to the target. The team with the ball closest to the target scores points. Multiple points can be scored with a single ball.

Games:

A game is generally played to 13 points, though this can vary based on local preferences.

Winning:

The team that reaches 13 points by scoring more points than the opponent wins the game.

Provençal Boule

Provençal Boule is similar to Provençal Pétanque, with some differences:

Teams:

Provençal Boule is usually played in teams of two players.

Objective:

The target is thrown at a distance between 15 meters and 20 meters, just like in Provençal Pétanque.

Throwing Circle:

A throwing circle is also used, and the player must have at least one foot in the circle when throwing.

Throwing the Balls:

Players throw their balls from behind the throwing circle, just as in Provençal Pétanque.

Scoring:

The goal is to place your balls as close as possible to the target to score points.

Games:

A game of Provençal Boule is usually played to 15 points.

Winning:

The team that reaches 15 points by scoring more points than the opponent wins the game.

Though Provençal Pétanque and Provençal Boule are similar games, they differ in the number of players per team, the number of points needed to win, and other specific rules.

Field Dimensions for Provençal Pétanque and Provençal Boule:

The dimensions for Provençal Pétanque and Provençal

Boule fields are generally the same, though there may be some local or competition-specific variations. Typical dimensions are:

Length:

The field should be at least 15 meters long, though shorter fields may be used for recreational play.

Width:

The field is generally about 4 meters wide.

Throwing Circle:

A 50-centimeter diameter throwing circle is marked on the ground, and the player's feet must be entirely inside this circle when throwing.

These dimensions are commonly used for both games, but it's important to note that they may vary based on specific competition rules or local preferences. When participating in a competition or playing on a specific field, always check the regulations to ensure compliance with the field dimensions.

Lyonnaise Boule

Objective:

The goal of Lyonnaise Boule is to place your balls as close as possible to the target (called "le but" or "le cochonnet") to score points.

Teams:

The game is usually played in teams of two players, called "doublettes," though individual games can also be played.

Field:

The playing field for Lyonnaise Boule is called "pas de tir." It measures about 27 meters long and 4 meters wide. It is covered with sand or a similar material.

Target:

The target is a small wooden ball, usually made of boxwood, measuring about 35 to 40 millimeters in diameter and weighing between 30 and 40 grams. The target is placed at the beginning of each end (round) by a team.

Throwing the Balls:

Each team has steel balls (usually two per player) which they must throw to place near the target. The balls typically weigh between 800 and 900 grams and measure about 90 to 100 millimeters in diameter.

Order of Play:

The team that won the previous end has the privilege of throwing the target and playing first.

Game Progress:

Each end progresses in several stages:

A player from the team with the privilege starts by throwing the target from a throwing circle at one end of the field.

Then, players from both teams take turns throwing their balls from the throwing circle towards the target, trying to place them as close as possible.

The team that places their balls closest to the target scores points. To score, the balls of a team must be closer to the target than all the balls of the other team.

End of the Game:

The game ends when one team reaches the predefined number of points needed to win the game. The required number of points varies based on local rules or the competition.

Lyonnaise Boule is a precision game that requires skill and strategy to optimally place the balls. The rules may vary slightly based on local traditions, but these basic rules form the foundation of Lyonnaise Boule.

Rules and Regulations According to the International Federation of Pétanque and Provençal Game (FIPJP) and National Pétanque Federations

Éric Borowiak, Journey to the Heart of Pétanque

Rules and Regulations According to the Internationale Federation of Pétanque and Provençal Game (FIPJP) and National Pétanque Federations

The game of pétanque is governed by official rules established by the Fédération Internationale de Pétanque et de Jeu Provençal (FIPJP) and national federations. These rules ensure fairness and sportsmanship during pétanque competitions. Here is a summary of the basic rules of the game:

Team Composition

The game can be played in singles (1 player against 1 player), doubles (2 players against 2 players), or triples (3 players against 3 players). Each player (or team) has three boules.

But (Cochonnet)

A small ball called "cochonnet" is thrown by a team at the beginning of the game. The cochonnet must be placed at a minimum distance from the throwing circle. The opposing players or teams then try to throw their boules as close as possible to the cochonnet.

Throw

The player throwing the boule (pointeur) must stand

inside the throwing circle and throw the boule towards the cochonnet. The player's foot must remain in the circle until the boule touches the ground. Other players of the same team, if they wish, can throw in turn. Players of the opposing team wait until all throws are completed.

Scoring

After all boules are thrown, the team with the closest boule to the cochonnet scores points. Each boule closer to the cochonnet than the best boule of the opposing team counts as one point. The game continues with a new round, where the winning team of the previous round throws the cochonnet.

Victory

The game is played until one team reaches a predetermined number of points (usually 13 or 15 points). The team that first reaches this number of points wins the game.

Other Rules

Boules can be thrown in different ways, including pointing (placing the boule close to the cochonnet) and shooting (hitting the opponent's boules to move them away). Players must respect fair play rules, including silence during the throw and respecting the order of play. In competitions, referees and officials ensure the rules are followed and resolve disputes.

These basic rules are common to most pétanque games, but there are regional variations and specific rules for certain tournaments or championships. It is advised to familiarize yourself with the specific rules of the event you are participating in.

Different Terrain Dimensions by Game Type and Competition Level

Éric Borowiak, Journey to the Heart of Pétanque

Different Dimensions of Courts Depending

on the Type of Game and Competition Level

The dimensions of pétanque courts can vary depending on the type of game and the level of competition for several reasons, including adapting the game to different contexts and skill levels. Here are some factors influencing these variations:

Level of Competition

Pétanque competitions are organized at different levels, from local tournaments to national and international competitions. The dimensions of the court can be adjusted to meet the standards and requirements specific to each level.

Type of Game

There are several variants of pétanque games, each with its own rules. For example, there is the singles game where teams face each other directly, and there is also the doubles game where two players team up. The dimensions of the court can be adapted to align with the specific rules of each variant.

Available Space

In many cases, the dimensions of the court depend on the available space in a given area. Some places may not have enough space for a standard pétanque court, and dimensions may be adjusted accordingly.

Local Traditions

In some regions, there may be local traditions regarding the dimensions of pétanque courts. These traditions may be based on specific historical or cultural preferences of a given community.

It is important to note that the Fédération Internationale de Pétanque et Jeu Provençal (FIPJP) issues official rules and standards for international pétanque competitions, including standard court dimensions. However, for local or amateur events, dimensions may vary based on the factors mentioned above.

Terrain Nature
by Game Variant

Éric Borowiak, Journey to the Heart of Pétanque

Terrain Nature

by Game Variant

The terrain is a crucial element in the game of pétanque. The characteristics of the terrain can significantly impact the course and outcome of a game. Here are some reasons why the terrain is important:

Playing Surface

The nature of the soil, whether hard, loose, grassy, or sandy, influences how the boules bounce and roll. Players must adapt to the surface to adjust their throwing technique.

Inclination and Relief

Terrains can have inclines or reliefs adding a strategic dimension to the game. Players must consider these characteristics to plan their throws and strategies.

Court Size

The court size can vary, influencing the distance between the boules and the cochonnet (the small wooden target ball). The dimensions of the court are regulated, but adjustments can be made depending on the circumstances.

Weather Conditions

Weather conditions, such as wind, rain, or sunshine, can also affect how the boules react. Players must consider these elements to adjust their technique.

Environment

The physical environment around the court, like the presence of obstacles or the layout of neighboring courts, can also impact game strategy.

The terrain in pétanque is important because it adds a strategic dimension to the game. Players must be able to adapt to different terrain conditions to succeed in their throws and develop effective strategies.

Different Terrains
by Game Type

Éric Borowiak, Journey to the Heart of Pétanque

Different Terrains

by Game Type

Classic pétanque Court:

Length:

The length of the court for a classic pétanque game must be at least 15 meters, although shorter courts may be used for recreational games.

Width:

The width of the court is generally around 4 meters.

Throwing Circle:

A 50-centimeter diameter circle is drawn on the ground, and the player's feet must be entirely within this circle when making their throw.

Junior pétanque Court:

The dimensions of the junior pétanque court can be reduced to accommodate younger players. For example, the length can be reduced to about 8 to 12 meters, and the width to about 2 to 3 meters.

Doublette pétanque Court:

When playing in doublette (two players per team), the court dimensions generally remain the same as for a classic game, that is, a length of at least 15 meters and a width of about 4 meters.

Tête-à-Tête pétanque Court:

Dimensions: In tête-à-tête (one player per team), the dimensions can be slightly reduced but generally remain similar to those of a classic game, with a length of at least 15 meters and a width of about 4 meters.

Triplette pétanque Court:

In triplette (three players per team), the dimensions are the same as for a classic game, with a length of at least 15 meters and a width of about 4 meters.

Official Competition pétanque Court:

For official competitions, the court dimensions must generally adhere to the specific rules of the Fédération Internationale de Pétanque et de Jeu Provençal (F.I.P.J.P.) or the Fédération Française de Pétanque et Jeu Provençal (F.F.P.J.P.).

Standard Dimensions: The standard dimensions are those mentioned for a classic game, but they can vary slightly depending on the tournament or championship rules.

It's important to note that these dimensions are generally used as guidelines, but they can vary depending on local preferences or the specific competition rules.

When participating in a competition or playing on a specific court, it is always recommended to check the current regulations to ensure compliance with the court dimensions.

Indoor and Outdoor Boulodromes

Éric Borowiak, Journey to the Heart of Pétanque

Indoor and Outdoor

Boulodromes

Boulodromes, whether indoor or outdoor, are facilities dedicated to the practice of pétanque and other boules games. Each type has its own unique characteristics and information.

Outdoor Boulodromes

Surface:

Outdoor boulodromes are generally set up in open-air on a flat surface, often fine gravel, sand, or synthetic terrain.

Facilities:

They can be equipped with multiple playing courts, each marked with lines indicating the throwing areas and required distances.

Cochonnet:

Outdoor boulodromes are designed to host games where the cochonnet can be placed at various distances, offering a variety of challenges.

Weather Conditions:

Games take place outdoors, exposed to weather

conditions. This adds an extra dimension to the game, asplayers must adapt to wind, rain, or sunshine variations.

Indoor Boulodromes

Surface:

Indoor boulodromes are set up inside specific buildings, often with a floor covering suitable for playing pétanque.

Lighting and Air Conditioning:

Unlike outdoor boulodromes, indoor facilities offer controlled lighting and air conditioning, creating more stable playing conditions.

Covered Court:

Indoor boulodromes allow for year-round play, regardless of outdoor weather conditions, which is an advantage in regions with harsh winters.

Competitions:

Some indoor boulodromes are used for official competitions and tournaments, providing a controlled environment for high-level events.

Common Features of Boulodromes:

Markings: Both types of boulodromes are often equipped with lines and circles on the ground to delimit the throwing areas and indicate distances.

Infrastructure:

Both types may include additional facilities such as stands, locker rooms, relaxation areas, and spectator stands.

In summary, whether outdoor or indoor, boulodromes are designed to provide a suitable environment for practicing pétanque, offering varied playing conditions and meeting the specific needs of players, from amateurs to competitors.

The Largest Boulodrome in France and the World

Éric Borowiak, Journey to the Heart of Pétanque

The Largest Boulodrome in
France and the World

The passion for pétanque in the Hauts-de-France region continues to grow, with a steady increase in the number of licensees each year. Thus, the city of Douai has embarked on an ambitious project for its new boulodrome, which turns out to be the largest in the world.

Nestled in the heart of the Ecoquartier du Raquet de Sin-le-Noble, this vast sports complex has been carefully designed to invigorate the area and provide residents with a place for leisure and social gatherings. Whether you are a pétanque enthusiast or an eminent champion, everyone can enjoy quality, welcoming, and warm facilities.

This colossal sports complex, entirely dedicated to pétanque, covers 8,000 square meters, offering boulistes over 190 playing lanes, including 128 outdoors. Inside the main building, 64 pétanque lanes are available to players, whether licensed or amateurs.

Fans of billon, a traditional game from the Nord-Pas-de-Calais, also have 2 dedicated lanes. In anticipation of major events, such as the 2023 French championship, the boulodrome includes a concrete stand with 1,000 seats facing the main court. In case of high attendance, two removable stands can be added to increase the capacity to

2,000 spectators.

The imposing dimensions of the building, measuring 180 meters long, up to 60 meters wide, and 14 meters high, illustrate the considerable ambition of the Douaisis agglomeration.

The Golden Bowl
of Petanque

Éric Borowiak, Journey to the Heart of Pétanque

The Golden Bowl

of pétanque

The second edition of the Bol d'Or, now a renowned tournament, took place on January 6 and 7, 2024, at the petanquodrome in Yssingeaux, a dynamic small town located in the Haute-Loire department in the Auvergne-Rhône-Alpes region, following the success of the previous edition in Le Puy-en-Velay in 2023.

Organized by Zvonko Radnic, world vice-champion, European champion, and multiple French champion in this discipline, recently also crowned club champion with his Arlanc team in 2022, this competition brought together 25 high-level teams from all over France, as well as two local teams, for this unique tournament.

After 24 hours of intense matches and 20 confrontations, the suspense reached its peak during the 21st and final match. Three triplettes were then vying for the final victory: Team RZ, led by Zvonko Radnic himself, Team France 2023, and Team Riviera.

It was ultimately Team France 2023 that won this final duel, leaving Team Riviera at the top of the standings thanks to a better specific goal average, despite Team RZ being the title holder and needing a victory to win the trophy again.

The event thus took place in an electric atmosphere at the Yssingeaux boulodrome, welcoming competitors from Saturday afternoon. Under the passionate eyes of the spectators, the players competed tirelessly, alternating day and night matches. Participants could rest in rooms set up near the courts before resuming play.

On Sunday morning, a general break was observed around a traditional meal, open to the public. During this rest period, Luc Debove, Meilleur Ouvrier de France Glacier and director of the École Nationale Supérieure de la Pâtisserie (ENSP) in Yssingeaux, created with his team an ice sculpture representing a champion of the discipline, accompanied by a tasting of local products.

Finally, the Telethon was associated with the event, with a public challenge whose proceeds were donated to this noble cause.

This exceptional weekend was marked by passion, intense matches, and conviviality, making the Bol d'Or an unmissable event for amateurs and professionals of this discipline. La Commère43, a well-recognized online journal, covered this event in detail.

https://www.lacommere43.fr

The Difference Between Boules and Pétanque

Éric Borowiak, Journey to the Heart of Pétanque

The Difference Between

Boule and pétanque

We do not play boules, Sir!

But pétanque!

Those who regularly practice this sport will tell you there is indeed a difference between "boule" and "pétanque." The boule refers to the spherical metal or wooden object used by players in various boules games, including pétanque. pétanque, on the other hand, is a specific sport that uses boules to play.

In other words, pétanque is a boules game where the objective is to throw your boules in a way that places them as close as possible to a small cochonnet (the cochonnet being a small target ball). The boule is the concrete object used to play pétanque, but the term "pétanque" refers to the entire sport and its rules.

Thus, in the context of pétanque, people often talk about "pétanque boules" to specifically refer to the boules used in this sport. Hence the expression "We do not play boules, Sir! But pétanque!" which highlights the fact that pétanque is a specific sport, distinct from the simple game of boules. This phrase emphasizes the pride and distinction of pétanque enthusiasts who consider their activity much more than a simple boules tossing game.

pétanque is a sport with its own rules, techniques, and traditions, and its enthusiasts like to highlight this specificity. It's a way to bring attention to the competitive and strategic aspect of pétanque compared to other activities that also use boules but may differ in their rules and objectives.

Various Ways to Play Pétanque

Éric Borowiak, Journey to the Heart of Pétanque

Various Ways to

Play Pétanque

There are different methods to play pétanque to meet the varied needs of players, account for environmental conditions, or experiment with fun variations of the traditional game.

One-on-One (Tête-à-Tête):

The term "one-on-one" refers to a game format where two players compete directly against each other. Unlike team games, such as doublette (two players per team) or triplette (three players per team), the one-on-one game pits one player against another.

In a one-on-one pétanque game, each player has three boules, aiming to score points by placing their boules as close as possible to the cochonnet (the small target ball) or by moving the opponent's boules. The player who first reaches a predetermined number of points wins the game.

This format is often used in pétanque competitions for individual and direct confrontations between players, adding an element of strategy and personal competition to the sport.

Triplette:

In pétanque, a "triplette" is a team composed of three

players. This is the most common team configuration in pétanque. Each player in the triplette has a specific role during the game, and the team's objective is to score points by throwing their pétanque boules as close as possible to the target (cochonnet) and preventing the opposing team from doing the same.

The traditional roles of the three players in a triplette are:

The Shooter (Tireur):

This player is generally skilled at shooting (hitting opponent's boules to move them away from the cochonnet) and playing offensively. The shooter's task is to clear the field of obstructive opponent's boules and score points with precise shooting.

The Pointer (Pointeur):

The pointer is responsible for placing the boules near the cochonnet, requiring great accuracy. This player must master distance and force to place the boules strategically.

The Middle (Milieu):

The middle plays a versatile role, alternating between shooting and pointing depending on the game's situation. This player supports both the shooter and the pointer by adapting to the team's needs.

The combination of these three roles allows the team to effectively manage different facets of the pétanque game, from precise pointing to strategic shooting. The choice of roles can vary depending on the individual skills of the players and the team strategy.

Triplette is one of the most popular forms of pétanque in competition, whether in amateur tournaments or professional levels. It requires good coordination among team members to successfully score points and defend their position on the field.

Doublette:

In pétanque, "doublette" means that two players team up to compete against another team of two players. This game configuration is common alongside the "triplette" (three players per team) and the "one-on-one" (two players competing individually).

Here's how a pétanque doublette game works:

Team Composition:

Each team consists of two players.

Boules per Player:

Each player has three boules.

Game Play:

The game starts with one team placing the cochonnet

(the small target ball). Teams then compete to place their boules as close as possible to the cochonnet while trying to disrupt the opponent's throws.

End of the Game:

The game ends depending on specific competition rules or player preferences. Two common scenarios are:

Reaching a Certain Number of Points:

In many doublette pétanque games, the team that first reaches a predetermined number of points wins (e.g., the first team to reach 13 points).

Playing a Fixed Number of Ends (Mènes):

In other competitions or informal games, the game can be played over a fixed number of ends (e.g., 10 ends). At the end of the last end, the team with the highest number of points wins.

The choice between these methods generally depends on the specific competition rules or the agreement between players before the game starts.

Specifications of Pétanque Boules

Éric Borowiak, Journey to the Heart of Pétanque

Specifications of
Pétanque Boules

There are specific standards and norms governing pétanque boules issued by the International Federation of Pétanque and Provençal Game (FIPJP), the international governing body for pétanque. These standards ensure fair play by establishing precise criteria for the characteristics of the boules. Here are some main specifications:

Hardness:

The hardness of pétanque boules refers to the material's resistance. It is measured on a specific scale, usually in Rockwell or Shore. Higher hardness values indicate harder boules, which tend to bounce less on the ground, useful for certain strategies. However, they might be less forgiving in precise placement.

Steels:

Pétanque boules are made from different types of steel, each with its own characteristics. Stainless steels are resistant to corrosion, while carbon steels are harder. The choice of steel can influence the boules' durability, grip, and impact resistance.

Diameters:

The diameter of a pétanque boule is its width

measurement. Boules come in different sizes, typically between 70 mm and 80 mm, although smaller and larger variations exist. The choice of diameter often depends on personal comfort and control preferences.

Weights:

The weight of pétanque boules can vary significantly, usually expressed in grams. Heavier boules tend to be more stable and resist opponent's boules better, beneficial for shooters. Lighter boules may be preferred by pointers for their maneuverability.

Striations:

The striations on the surface of pétanque boules are grooves or raised patterns that help improve grip and spin when thrown. Striations can vary in shape and depth, and some players prefer them for better adherence and control during throws.

These characteristics are essential for choosing the pétanque boules that best suit your playing style and personal preferences. Understanding these elements will help you make informed decisions when purchasing your pétanque boules and improve your performance on the field.

Stainless Steel (Inox) Boules:

When talking about "stainless steel boules," it means the boule is entirely made of high-quality stainless steel, from the core to the outer surface. This characteristic is particularly appreciated by many pétanque players for several reasons:

Durability:

Stainless steel pétanque boules are known for their durability. Stainless steel is resistant to corrosion and wear, ensuring the boules remain in good condition for many years, even with regular use.

Reduced Maintenance:

Stainless steel boules are easy to maintain. They typically only require occasional cleaning to stay in good condition.

Stability and Consistency:

Stainless steel boules offer stability and consistency in play, as they retain their weight and hardness characteristics over time.

Aesthetic Appeal:

Stainless steel has a shiny and elegant appearance, attractive to many players. However, it's important to note that stainless steel boules can be heavier than boules made from other materials, influencing the player's choice depending on their playing style.

Some players prefer lighter boules for pointing, while others favor heavier boules for shooting.

Ultimately, choosing a stainless steel pétanque boule depends on the player's preferences and playing style. It's one of the many options available to meet pétanque players' needs.

Carbon Steel Boules:

Carbon steel is a common material used for manufacturing pétanque boules. It is a type of steel primarily composed of iron and carbon, with a small amount of other elements. Here are some important characteristics of carbon steel for pétanque boules:

Hardness:

Carbon steel is generally harder than other materials used for pétanque boules, providing high resistance to wear.

Weight:

Carbon steel pétanque boules can be manufactured in a range of weights to suit players' preferences.

Durability:

Due to its hardness, carbon steel is durable and resistant to shocks and damage.

Finish:

Carbon steel pétanque boules are usually subjected to a surface treatment, such as a chrome or nickel coating, to improve their appearance and resistance to corrosion.

Cost:

Carbon steel pétanque boules are often more affordable than those made from other materials, making them popular among casual players.

Carbon steel is a popular choice for pétanque boules because of its robustness and durability. However, it may require regular maintenance to avoid corrosion, especially if used outdoors. Many manufacturers apply surface treatments to protect carbon steel boules.

To be authorized in official competitions, pétanque boules must undergo approval by the International and French Federations of Pétanque and Provençal Game (FIPJP and FFPJP), after meeting all the specifications of their standards.

Pétanque boules are available in different configurations based on player preferences and competition regulations.

Here are some details:

Solid Boules:

Some pétanque boules are solid, meaning they are not hollow inside. These boules can be made from stainless steel, carbon steel, or other materials. They are often used by players who prefer a higher weight and a particular playing feel.

Hollow Boules:

Other pétanque boules are hollow inside. They can also be made from stainless steel, carbon steel, or other materials. These boules are appreciated for their lightness and maneuverability.

Boules with Steel Weights:

Some boules, typically used in specific competitions, may have a steel weight inside. This means they contain an added steel material to increase their weight. These boules are often used in specific playing conditions where a precise weight is required.

The choice of pétanque boules depends on the player's preferences in terms of weight, playing feel, and style of play. It's important to comply with the specific regulations of the tournament or competition in which you participate, as some competitions may have particular requirements for boules.

Shooting
Distances

Éric Borowiak, Journey to the Heart of Pétanque

Shooting Distances

In pétanque, skillful management of shooting distances is crucial for strategic play. Players constantly need to accurately evaluate the distance between their boules and the cochonnet to optimize their throws. Here are the main principles and techniques to consider for successful shooting distances in pétanque:

Distance Assessment:

Accurately evaluating distances is the basis of effective play. Players must develop the ability to measure distances visually or using specific tools, like measuring tapes, to determine the position of boules relative to the cochonnet.

Throw Control:

Adjusting the force and trajectory of the throw according to distance is essential. For short distances, a more precise and controlled throw is necessary, while longer distances require a more powerful throw.

Terrain Analysis:

Taking the terrain into account is crucial. Uneven or sloping surfaces can influence the trajectory of the boule. Players need to adjust their technique accordingly to achieve the desired distances.

Practice and Experience:

Mastering shooting distances requires regular practice and experience. Players improve their skills by repeating throws and learning from mistakes.

Strategic Choice:

Players must also make strategic decisions based on distances. For instance, choosing to point a boule close to the cochonnet or trying to displace an opponent's boule depends on the assessed distance.

Shooting distances in pétanque play a crucial role in success and strategy. Players who develop their ability to evaluate distances accurately and adjust their throws accordingly gain a significant advantage in the game. Regular practice and analysis of playing conditions are essential to honing these skills.

Throwing
the Jack

Éric Borowiak, Journey to the Heart of Pétanque

Throwing the

Jack

The distance at which you must throw the jack at the start of a pétanque game depends on the specific rules of the competition or the players' preferences. However, there are general guidelines for jack throwing distance:

Short Distance:

In many informal or leisure pétanque games, the jack is thrown at a relatively short distance, typically between 6 and 10 meters from the throwing area. This distance allows players to start the game close to each other and promotes more precise throws.

Medium Distance:

For more competitive games or those following official rules, the jack throwing distance is often set between 6 and 10 meters, or even more. The exact distance is usually determined by an agreement between the teams before the game starts or according to specific tournament rules.

Long Distance:

In some competitions or to add an extra challenge, the jack can be thrown at a longer distance, sometimes up to 15 meters or more. This makes the game more difficult as players need to make stronger and more accurate throws to place their boules near the jack.

It is important to note that regardless of the chosen distance, it must be the same for all ends in the game. Players must respect the established jack throwing distance at the beginning of the game or tournament. Specific rules may vary, so make sure to check the regulations for the competition you are participating in.

Rule Compliance:

Failure to comply with the throwing circle rules can result in penalties, including the loss of points or disqualification of the player or team.

The throwing circle is an essential element of pétanque as it ensures that all players adhere to equal conditions and do not gain any undue advantage during throws. This helps maintain the integrity and fairness of the game, which is crucial in this competitive sport.

Preparation for the Pétanque Throw

Éric Borowiak, Journey to the Heart of Pétanque

Preparing for the Pétanque Throw

Preparation for the pétanque throw is crucial for ensuring a good shot or point. Here are the steps to follow to prepare for the pétanque throw:

Choosing the Boule:

Select the pétanque boule that best suits the situation. Boules vary in weight, diameter, hardness, and striations. A heavier boule is generally used for shooting, while a lighter boule is preferable for pointing. The hardness and striations depend on personal preferences.

Observing the Situation:

Before throwing, assess the situation on the field. Examine the position of the opponent's boules, the location of the jack, and the field conditions (ground, obstacles, etc.).

Choosing the Target:

Decide whether you will point (try to place your boule near the jack) or shoot (try to displace an opponent's boule or the jack). Select your target accordingly.

Positioning:

Position yourself behind the throwing line, with your feet firmly anchored to the ground as explained earlier.

Make sure you have a clear view of the target.

Concentration:

Take a few moments to mentally focus on your shot or point. Mentally visualize your boule reaching the target with precision.

Grip the Boule:

Hold the pétanque boule correctly according to your preferred grip technique. Ensure the boule is clean and dry for a good grip.

Breathing:

Take a deep breath to relax. Controlling your breathing can help reduce stress and improve accuracy.

Smooth Movement:

Initiate the throw with a smooth arm movement. The speed of the arm will depend on the type of throw you are making (point or shoot).

Follow-Through:

After releasing the boule, make sure to follow through by keeping your eyes on the target. A good follow-through can help you adjust your shot in real-time.

Practice:

Practice regularly to improve your technique. The more

you practice, the better you will develop your sense of throwing and accuracy.

Strategy:

Remember that strategy is important. Communicate with your teammates to decide on the best approach based on the game situation.

Fair Play:

Respect the rules and practice fair play. Congratulate your opponents on their good shots and be respectful, whether you win or lose.

Mental preparation and technique are essential for succeeding in pétanque. By combining these steps with regular practice, you will improve your skills over time.

Aiming Properly for the Pétanque Throw

Éric Borowiak, Journey to the Heart of Pétanque

Aiming Properly for

the Pétanque Throw

Aiming in a pétanque throw is a crucial skill for hitting your target, whether it is the jack or an opponent's boule. Here's how to properly aim in a pétanque throw:

Choose Your Target:

Clearly identify the boule or jack you want to hit. This may vary depending on your game strategy, whether you are aiming to place near the jack or shoot an opponent's boule.

Find Your Aiming Line:

Mentally visualize an imaginary line between your boule and your target. This line will guide the trajectory your boule needs to follow to reach the target.

Align Your Body:

Position yourself so that your body is aligned with the aiming line. This means your shoulders, hips, and feet should be oriented in the direction of your target.

Fix Your Gaze:

Focus your gaze on the target while maintaining intense concentration. Your eyes should stay fixed on the target throughout the throwing process.

Prepare Your Throw:

Hold the boule comfortably in your hand, ready to be thrown. Your arm should be bent at a natural angle to allow you to throw the boule with precision.

Visualize the Throw:

Before throwing the boule, mentally visualize the trajectory you want it to follow to reach the target. Imagine the perfect throw.

Throw the Boule:

Execute your throwing motion while keeping in mind the trajectory you visualized. Use appropriate force and precision depending on the distance to the target.

Follow Your Throw:

After releasing the boule, follow its trajectory with your eyes to see if it gets close to the target. This can help you make adjustments to your future throws.

Analyze and Adjust:

If your throw did not hit the target as intended, consider the field conditions, wind strength, boule quality, etc. Use this information to adjust your next throw.

Practice Regularly:

Aiming is one of the most important aspects of pétanque and requires time and training to master fully.

With regular practice, you will become a better aimer and increase your chances of success on the field.

The Pétanque
Throw

Éric Borowiak, Journey to the Heart of Pétanque

The Pétanque

Throw

Throwing the boule in pétanque is a crucial technique in the game. Here's how to execute a basic pétanque throw:

How to Position Yourself for a Pétanque Throw?

Your position as a player is crucial for ensuring precision and effectiveness. Here's how to position yourself:

Foot Position:

Start by positioning yourself behind the throwing line with your feet firmly anchored to the ground. Your back foot (the one opposite your dominant hand if you are right-handed, or the same side if you are left-handed) should be slightly back, while your front foot is slightly forward. This position allows for good balance and rotation of the upper body during the throw.

Weight Distribution:

Most of your body weight should be on your back foot. The front foot serves as a support and direction point, but stability mainly comes from the back foot. Keep the weight evenly distributed between both feet to avoid leaning forward during the throw.

Body Position:

Stand straight with your torso slightly leaning forward. Your gaze should be fixed on the target (the jack or the boule you are aiming for). Ensure that your dominant shoulder (the one on your throwing hand side) is oriented towards the target.

Hand Position:

Hold the pétanque boule in your dominant hand using your preferred grip technique (flat, pinch, etc.). The non-dominant hand (support hand) can be placed under the boule for better control. Keep the boule at hip level, near your thigh, during the throw.

Throwing:

For the throw itself, release the boule with a smooth and steady arm movement. Ensure to follow through the throw to maintain accuracy. Your back foot can slightly pivot forward during the throw to aid the body's rotation.

Respecting the Rules:

Finally, make sure to respect the game rules, particularly staying behind the throwing line until your boule has touched the ground. Remember that the order of throws may vary depending on the game strategy (pointing, shooting, etc.).

Player positioning can vary slightly from one player

toanother based on personal style, but these general tips should help you develop a solid stance to improve your pétanque game.

Following the
Boule in Pétanque

Éric Borowiak, Journey to the Heart of Pétanque

Following the Boule

in Pétanque

"Following through" in pétanque refers to the action of tracking the trajectory of the boule after it has been thrown. It is a crucial step to evaluate the accuracy of your throw and determine if the boule is approaching the intended target, whether it is the jack or an opponent's boule.

Analyzing the Trajectory:

By following the trajectory of the boule, you can judge if it is heading towards the desired spot. If not, you can take measures to correct your next throw. For instance, if the boule veers too far to the left, you might decide to aim slightly to the right on your next shot.

Understanding Field Conditions:

Following through also helps you better understand how the field surface influences the boule's trajectory. If you notice the boule bouncing or deviating due to irregularities on the field, you can take this into account in your next throws.

Communication and Strategy:

In doubles or team competitions, following through is essential for communication between teammates. It allows for discussing the next shots, necessary adjustments, and strategies to adopt.

In summary, following through is an integral part of the pétanque playing process. It helps you adjust your throws based on previous results, better understand the field, and improve your accuracy over time.

Throwing the boule in pétanque requires practice to become precise and effective. Each player develops their technique over time. Feel free to play regularly to refine your skills.

Tips for Improving
at Pétanque

Éric Borowiak, Journey to the Heart of Pétanque

Tips for Improving at Pétanque

To improve at pétanque, regular practice is essential. The more you play, the more you refine your skills. Dedicate time to both shooting and pointing, the two fundamental skills of the game.

Shooting Practice: Precision and practice are key. Target different distances and perfect your ability to execute accurate shots. Simultaneously, work on pointing to strategically place your boules near the jack.

Observation: Watch more experienced players to learn from their movements and strategies. Adapt your play based on the type of terrain you're playing on and develop a deep understanding of the official pétanque rules.

Team Communication: If you play in a team, communicate effectively with your teammates. Develop collective strategies and understand each other's roles in different game situations.

Stress Management:

Staying focused and calm is crucial, even in challenging situations. After each game, analyze your performance, identify mistakes, and learn from your experiences.

Physical Condition:

Do not neglect your physical fitness. Pétanque requires a certain level of endurance and good balance. Combining these tips with a positive attitude and a constant willingness to improve will significantly enhance your pétanque game.

Shooting in Pétanque

Éric Borowiak, Journey to the Heart of Pétanque

Shooting in

Pétanque

In pétanque, "tirer" refers to the action of throwing a boule with the intent to hit one or more opponent's boules or the jack (the small target object) to move or eliminate them from the playing area. Shooting is often used to eliminate opponent's boules that are well positioned near the jack to score points or regain an advantage in the game.

When a player decides to shoot, they must aim precisely to hit the desired target, whether it is an opponent's boule or the jack. Shooting typically requires greater force and precision than other types of throws, such as pointing (placing your boule near the jack without touching the opponent's boules).

Shooting is a crucial skill in pétanque, and experienced players often develop specific techniques for executing precise and strategic shots. It is an important part of the game's strategy, as a successful shot can change the course of a game in your favor.

Foot Placement in Pétanque

There are different ways to position your feet in pétanque:

The foot at right angles:

The feet are placed side by side, parallel to the throwing line, with a slight heel opening to maintain balance. This position is often used for precision throws, such as scoring.

Foot forward:

One foot (usually the one opposite your dominant hand) is slightly forward. The back foot is placed behind the throwing line, while the front foot is slightly in front of the line. This position allows the player to throw the ball with a higher trajectory to shoot or overcome obstacles.

Glued feet:

The feet are placed together, side by side, the heels almost touching. This stance is used for accurate shots but can also be used for hard shots if the player feels comfortable in this stance.

Spread Feet:

Feet are spread at a comfortable distance, slightly wider than shoulder-width apart. Both feet are parallel to the throwing line. This position offers maximum stability, useful for powerful shots or when the player needs to maintain a solid stance.

Each pétanque player develops their own foot

placement preference based on their playing style and personal technique. It is important to choose the position that allows you to throw with the most precision and control. Additionally, always respect the game rules, particularly staying behind the throwing line until your boule has touched the ground.

The Rétropissette

Éric Borowiak, Journey to the Heart of Pétanque

The Rétropissette

The "rétropissette" in pétanque refers to a particular technique used by players to move boules already in play. This technique involves shooting your own boule with enough force so that it bounces off an obstacle (such as the edge of the field) before returning towards the opponent's boules.

The idea behind the rétropissette is to create a rebound effect that can disrupt the arrangement of the opponent's boules and potentially move them away from the jack (the small target ball players aim for).

It is an audacious strategy that can change the course of a game but also carries risks, as the boule can also return towards the shooting team's boules. However, depending on the competitions and federations, specific rules regarding the use of the rétropissette may vary. Generally, it is allowed in many tournaments and competitions as long as the general rules of pétanque are respected.

Therefore, players are recommended to familiarize themselves with the specific rules of the competition they are participating in to ensure the rétropissette is permitted and understand any potential restrictions that may be in place.

In summary, the rétropissette is a particular shooting technique in pétanque that involves a rebound of the boule on an obstacle to disrupt the arrangement of the opponent's boules on the field.

The Boule
Grip

Éric Borowiak, Journey to the Heart of Pétanque

The Grip of
the Boule

The grip refers to how you hold and maintain the pétanque boule in your hand before and during the throw. It is crucial for ensuring precise control of the boule and minimizing errors during the throw. Here are some tips to achieve an optimal grip on the pétanque boule:

Comfortable Grip:

Ensure the boule rests comfortably in your hand, eliminating any risk of slipping or unnecessary movement during the throw.

Preferred Technique:

The way you hold the boule depends on your personal technique. Different grip methods exist, such as the three-finger grip (thumb, index, and middle finger), the two-finger grip (thumb and middle finger), or other variations. Choose the one that suits you best.

Equal Finger Placement:

The fingers should evenly surround the boule without exerting excessive pressure. Keep the fingers slightly curved to hold the boule in place.

Comfortable and Dry:

Ensure the grip is comfortable and does not cause pain or tension in the hand. Avoid a wet or slippery boule, as a damp boule can be challenging to control.

Consistency:

Try to maintain the same pressure and finger placement on each throw. Consistency in the grip can contribute to improved accuracy.

Adjust for Balance:

Some players adjust the position of their fingers to balance the boule, so it spins evenly during the throw.

Situation-Dependent:

Your grip may vary based on the game situation. For example, a firmer grip can be used for shooting, while a lighter grip might be preferred for pointing.

The essential point is to find a grip that ensures maximum control over the boule while remaining comfortable for you. Preferences for grip techniques can vary from player to player, so feel free to experiment with different methods to discover what works best for you. Regular practice will help you perfect your grip technique over time.

Striated
Pétanque

Éric Borowiak, Journey to the Heart of Pétanque

Striated Pétanque Boules

A striated pétanque boule has grooves or raised lines on its surface. These striations are intentionally added during the boule's manufacturing for several benefits:

Improved Grip:

They enhance the grip between the boule and the player's hand, which can be particularly useful in wet conditions or when hands are sweaty.

Better Control:

The striations offer better control over the boule's rotation during the throw, allowing the player to influence the boule's trajectory and add extra effect.

Aesthetics:

Some players prefer the aesthetics of striated boules. The use of striated boules depends on individual player preferences, and official pétanque rules generally do not impose specific restrictions on this aspect, as long as the boules meet the weight and diameter standards.

Indoor Play Area

Éric Borowiak, Journey to the Heart of Pétanque

Indoor Playing

Area

Traditionally, pétanque is an outdoor game played on sandy or gravel fields. However, it can be interesting to play pétanque indoors for several reasons:

Weather Conditions:

In some regions, the climate can be an obstacle to regular outdoor pétanque practice. Bad weather, cold, or excessive heat can make it difficult to hold games outdoors. Playing indoors avoids these weather constraints.

Winter Season:

During the winter months, it can be difficult to play pétanque outdoors due to snow, frost, or unfavorable weather conditions. Indoor play allows you to maintain pétanque practice throughout the year.

Accessibility:

Some places do not have suitable outdoor facilities for pétanque, or the outdoor fields may be occupied. Indoor facilities offer an accessible alternative available at any time.

Events and Competitions:

Organizing pétanque tournaments or competitions indoors can be more practical, especially if outdoor space is limited. It also allows attracting a broader audience and organizing events throughout the year.

New Game Formats:

The indoor environment offers the possibility to experiment with new game formats, with rules adapted to the available space. This can include variations of traditional pétanque or specific rules for the indoor environment.

Consistent Lighting and Playing Conditions:

Indoors, lighting is usually more controllable, ensuring consistent playing conditions. This can contribute to a fairer and more predictable gaming experience.

Ease of Organization:

Organizing an indoor pétanque game can be easier in terms of logistics, particularly regarding the availability of fields and tournament organization.

Indoor Playing Style

Éric Borowiak, Journey to the Heart of Pétanque

Indoor Playing

Style

While the fundamental idea remains the same as playing outdoors, adapting the conditions when opting for indoor play is necessary.

Required Space:

You will need an open and flat space of at least 12 meters long and 4 meters wide for a standard pétanque field. Dimensions can vary depending on the space available.

Surface:

The field should be covered with a solid material, such as sand or clay. The material should be leveled to ensure fair play.

Throwing Circle:

Mark a throwing circle with a diameter of 50 centimeters at a distance of 6 to 10 meters from the throwing line.

Throwing Line:

Draw a throwing line at least 1 meter behind the throwing circle. Players must stay behind this line when throwing their boules.

Jack (cochonnet):

Place the jack in the center of the field, at a distance of at least 6 meters from the throwing circle.

Once you have set up your pétanque field, you can play by following the basic rules of pétanque. Here is a brief overview of the rules:

Each player or team has boules they throw to get close to the jack.

The player or team that places their boule closest to the jack wins the round.

The game continues until a certain number of points is reached or a specific number of rounds have been played, depending on the competition's specific rules.

Players must throw their boules while staying behind the throwing line.

Opponents can shoot (hit the opponent's boules to move them away from the jack) or point (attempt to place their boules as close as possible to the jack) to score points.

Excluding a Player from a Pétanque Game

Éric Borowiak, Journey to the Heart of Pétanque

Exclusing a player from

a Pétanque Game

The smooth running of a pétanque game relies on the adherence to rules and sporting behavior. Excluding a player may be considered when certain rules are not respected, highlighting the importance of fair play in this popular game.

Firstly, unsporting behavior can be a potential cause for exclusion. If a player adopts an aggressive or inappropriate attitude or insults their opponents, they may be excluded from the game. This also includes disputes and non-compliance with the referee's decisions, which go against the ethics of the game.

Additionally, deliberate non-compliance with game rules is another reason for exclusion. Actions such as stepping outside the throwing circle, incorrect throws, or refusing to comply with referee decisions can result in a penalty.

Excessive delay during the game can also lead to a player's exclusion. Pétanque games generally have strict timing for each throw, and a player who takes too long may disrupt the game's flow and face exclusion.

The consumption of alcohol or drugs on the pétanque field may be prohibited, and a player under the influence of these substances, thereby disrupting the game's smooth running, may also be excluded.

Finally, cheating in any form, such as subtly changing balls or manipulating their placement, is a serious infraction that can lead to the exclusion of the guilty player.

It's important to note that the decision to exclude a player should be made by a referee or game official in strict accordance with the competition rules or specific rules established before the start of the game. Excluding a player is generally a last resort, and resolving conflicts through dialogue and adherence to game rules remains the best approach.

Choosing Your Pétanque Boules

Éric Borowiak, Journey to the Heart of Pétanque

Choosing Your

Pétanque Boules

Choosing your pétanque boules is crucial as it can significantly impact your performance and enjoyment of the game. Here are some tips for selecting the right pétanque boules:

Determine Your Playing Style:

Think about your preferred playing style. Are you more of a pointer (aiming to place your boules near the jack) or a shooter (aiming to dislodge opponents' boules or point precisely)? Your playing style can influence the type of boules you need.

Consider Weight and Size:

Pétanque boules come in different sizes and weights. Heavier boules can be more stable and better suited for shooters, while lighter boules are often preferred by pointers. Try different sizes and weights to find what suits you best.

Choose the Material:

Pétanque boules are generally made of steel, stainless steel, carbon, or resin. Steel or stainless steel boules are durable and suitable for intensive use. Carbon boules are lightweight, ideal for pointing. Resin boules are an economical choice and suitable for beginners.

Try Before Buying:

If possible, try several boules of different models and weights to feel their grip. Many pétanque stores have trial fields to allow players to test boules before purchasing.

Consult Experts:

If you are new to choosing pétanque boules, don't hesitate to seek advice from more experienced players or specialists in stores. They can guide you based on your skill level and preferences.

Consider Your Budget:

Pétanque boules are available in a wide price range. Set a budget before buying and look for quality options that fit your means.

Ultimately, the choice of your pétanque boules will depend on your personal preferences and playing style. It can be helpful to try several boules before making a final choice. Investing in good pétanque boules can improve your game and your enjoyment of this convivial sport.

Maintaining Your Pétanque Boules and Preventing Oxidation

Éric Borowiak, Journey to the Heart of Pétanque

Maintaining Your Pétanque
Boules and Preventing Oxidation

Regular maintenance of your pétanque boules is essential to ensure their longevity and maintain their performance. Here are general steps to maintain your pétanque boules:

Clean Your Boules Regularly:

After each game, thoroughly wipe your boules with a dry cloth to remove dirt, dust, and moisture. Do not leave them dirty or wet for an extended period.

Use a Chamois:

A chamois cloth (soft leather cloth) is ideal for wiping your boules. It gently cleans the surface without scratching it.

Avoid Contact with Rough Surfaces:

When playing, avoid throwing your boules on abrasive or rough terrains, as this could damage the surface.

Check the Condition of Your Boules:

Regularly inspect your boules for any damage, scratches, or oxidation spots. Treat them immediately if necessary.

Store Your Boules Properly:

Use a pétanque bag or case to store your boules when not in use. Ensure they are protected from moisture and dirt.

Avoid Contact with Corrosive Substances:

Keep your boules away from contact with corrosive chemicals or liquids that could damage them.

Regular Maintenance:

Make a habit of regularly maintaining your boules to keep them in good condition.

By following these maintenance and prevention tips, you should be able to extend the lifespan of your pétanque boules while reducing the risk of oxidation.

Oil, a Protective Substance for Your Boules

Éric Borowiak, Journey to the Heart of Pétanque

Oil, a Protective Substance

for Your Boules

Proper maintenance of pétanque boules is essential to ensure their longevity and prevent rust formation. A common practice is regular oiling, which creates a thin protective layer on the metal surface, protecting against oxidation from moisture and air.

For frequent users, it is recommended to apply non-food oil after each game, although some prefer to do it weekly or monthly, depending on usage frequency. Opt for oil specifically designed for pétanque boules, usually a light mineral oil like vaseline oil, which forms a protective layer without leaving sticky residues.

Apply the oil evenly on the boule surface using a clean, soft cloth, ensuring thorough coverage. Some prefer using a small brush to reach the grooves and stripes of the boule.

After letting the oil act for a few hours or overnight, gently wipe off any excess oil with a clean cloth to prevent the boules from becoming too slippery during play.

Consider the specifics of modern pétanque boules, which may have a particular coating. In some cases, oiling is unnecessary and might even impair their performance. Always follow the manufacturer's recommendations for optimal maintenance without compromising boule quality.

Personalized Engraving

Éric Borowiak, Journey to the Heart of Pétanque

Personalized

Engraving

Many pétanque players choose to have personalized engravings on their boules for several reasons:

Easy Identification:

Personalization allows players to easily identify their boules among others, especially when multiple boules are near the jack.

Playing Preferences:

Some players have specific preferences regarding the weight, size, texture, or type of boules. Personalized engraving ensures each boule meets the player's preferences.

Personal Style:

Players often like to add a personal touch to their equipment. They can choose designs, symbols, or messages that reflect their personality or playing style.

Gifts and Souvenirs:

Personalized pétanque boules make excellent gifts for friends, family, or teammates. They can also serve as souvenirs for special events or tournaments.

Sense of Ownership:

Owning personalized pétanque boules can enhance a player's sense of ownership and pride in their equipment.

Ease of Replacement:

In case of loss or theft, personalized boules are easier to identify and recover.

Sponsorship:

In competitions or sponsored tournaments, players may choose to have their sponsor's logo or name engraved on their boules.

Ultimately, personalizing pétanque boules offers practical and personal benefits to players. It creates a special bond between the player and their equipment while making it easier to identify the boules on the playing field.

Essential Equipment for Pétanque Players

Éric Borowiak, Journey to the Heart of Pétanque

Essential Equipment

for Pétanque Players

Pétanque is a simple and accessible sport, but it does require some basic equipment to play correctly. Here is the essential equipment for pétanque players:

Pétanque Boules:

Pétanque boules, also known as "boules," are the central element of the game. Each player or team typically has a set of three boules. The boules are made of metal, often stainless steel, and come in various sizes and weights. The choice of boules depends on individual player preferences in terms of weight, size, and texture.

Magnet for Picking Up Boules:

Using a magnet to pick up pétanque boules is a practical tip widely adopted by many players. These magnets, often attached to a cord, are specially designed to attract the metal boules, making it easier to pick them up without constantly bending over.

The main advantage of this method lies in the ease of picking up boules. By avoiding the need to continuously bend down, the magnet makes the process smoother, saving effort and time. This allows players to focus more on the game itself rather than the tedious task of picking up scattered boules.

Besides saving time, using a magnet can help reduce the risk of injury by avoiding repetitive bending movements. This is particularly beneficial during prolonged games where frequent picking up could lead to back strain or pain.

It is recommended to ensure that the magnet used is powerful enough to attract the pétanque boules. Additionally, in official competitions, it is prudent to check local rules or specific tournament regulations to confirm that using a magnet is allowed. In summary, using a magnet is a practical and efficient method for simplifying the task of picking up pétanque boules on the field.

The Jack (Cochonnet):

The jack, also known as the target ball, is a small ball used as the central target in pétanque. Traditionally made of wood, resin, or metal, the jack has a diameter that should be between 25 and 35 millimeters and a weight ranging from 10 to 18 grams according to official rules.

At the beginning of the game, a player throws the jack to a predetermined distance on the playing field. Other players then try to throw their boules as close as possible to the jack. The often white or yellow color of the jack makes it easy to spot on the field.

Besides its role as the central point around which the game revolves, the jack is crucial for determining which players or teams score points. Boules that are closer to the jack than those of the opponent accumulate points.

The jack adds a strategic dimension to the pétanque game, influencing the players' tactics regarding the placement of their boules on the field and thus making the game more engaging and competitive.

Measuring Tape:

A measuring tape is used to determine which boule is closest to the jack when there is uncertainty. It is a flexible tape or band, often retractable, used to measure the distance between the boules and the jack.

When there are boules very close to each other, and it is difficult to visually determine which is closest to the jack, players can use the measuring tape for a precise measurement. Here is how it works:

The player gently pulls the tape or band of the measuring tape to extend it.

They place the end of the measuring tape at a reference point on the boule closest to the jack.

While holding the end of the measuring tape on this boule, the player can measure the distance to all other boules to determine which is closest to the jack.

The boule closest to the jack is considered the winner for the round.

The measuring tape is a simple but useful tool to resolve situations where there is doubt about which boule is closest. It ensures fair play in pétanque.

Throwing Circle:

A throwing circle in pétanque is a circular area on the ground where the player must stand when making a throw (shoot or point) during a game. The throwing circle is a fundamental rule in pétanque to ensure fair and regulated play.

The throwing circle is usually drawn on the ground, either naturally in dirt or gravel or with a metal or plastic circle placed on the ground. The diameter of the throwing circle is generally about 50 centimeters, though this may vary according to specific tournament or pétanque federation rules.

The player must have at least one foot (or both feet, according to local rules) inside the throwing circle when throwing. The player cannot exceed or step over the circle limit during the throw.

Transport Bag:

While it is not strictly necessary to have a specific bag or case for transporting your pétanque boules, using such an accessory is often recommended for several practical reasons.

Firstly, a dedicated case can offer extra protection for your boules, preserving them from shocks and scratches during transport. Moreover, these bags usually have handles or a shoulder strap, making them easier to carry.

By opting for a bag designed specifically for pétanque boules, you can also benefit from additional features, such as special compartments for storing jacks, cleaning cloths, or other necessary accessories during the game. This contributes to better organization and preparation before each game. Additionally, pétanque-specific bags are often made of durable materials, ensuring the bag's longevity. This not only guarantees adequate protection for your boules but also provides a reliable long-term transport solution.

However, if you prefer an alternative, you can use a sports bag or any suitable bag. The essential thing is to ensure that your boules are well-protected and that transport is convenient for you.

Cap:

While wearing a cap is not mandatory when playing pétanque, it can be an option to consider depending on the conditions and individual preferences.

A cap can offer protection against direct sun exposure, helping to avoid sunburn and maintain a feeling of coolness on sunny days. Practically, a cap can also reduce sun glare, improving visual comfort during the game. Additionally, it can help control sweat by absorbing it, which can be particularly useful in preventing sweat from running into the eyes.

However, wearing a cap remains largely a matter of personal preference. Some players may prefer to play without a cap, while others may consider it a comfortable accessory or a matter of style. Ultimately, the choice of whether to wear a cap while playing pétanque will depend on your individual preferences and the weather conditions at the time of the game.

Cleaning Cloth:

To clean your pétanque boules, it is recommended to use a soft, non-abrasive cloth. A microfiber or chamois cloth is often an excellent choice, as it is gentle on the boule's surface while effectively removing dirt, dust, and any grass or terrain residue.

Avoid using rough cloths, metal brushes, or other abrasive materials that could damage the surface of the boules. The goal of cleaning is to preserve the quality and texture of the boule while simply removing impurities.

If the boules are very dirty, you can also use warm water and mild soap. However, make sure to dry the boules thoroughly after cleaning to avoid any risk of rust, especially if the boules are made of stainless steel.

Shoes:

While it is not mandatory to have specific shoes to play pétanque, choosing appropriate footwear can significantly enhance the playing experience.

Shoes with a non-slip sole offer better traction on the playing field, which is particularly beneficial when shooting and moving around. Opting for comfortable, well-fitting shoes that provide good support can reduce fatigue and improve comfort during long games.

Depending on the surface you are playing on (sand, gravel, etc.), suitable shoes for the terrain can also be advantageous. Additionally, the lateral stability offered by some shoes can help prevent slips and injuries.

It is also recommended to check local regulations or specific event rules, as some official competitions may have specific rules regarding the type of shoes allowed. Thus, while specific shoes are not strictly necessary, choosing suitable footwear can certainly improve your pétanque playing experience.

With these pétanque essentials, you will be ready to face every game with confidence, comfort, and precision. So, prepare your equipment, invite your friends, and enjoy unforgettable moments under the sun during your pétanque games.

Official Pétanque Attire (for Competitions)

Éric Borowiak, Journey to the Heart of Pétanque

Official Pétanque Attire

(for Competitions)

In pétanque, there is generally no strict dress code for competitions, unlike some more formal sports. However, it is important to present oneself with decency, cleanliness, and respect towards other players and the public during official competitions. Here are some guidelines on appropriate attire for pétanque competitions:

Clean and Decent Clothing:

Wear clean and decent clothing. Avoid torn, dirty, or inappropriate clothing. Opt for comfortable clothes that allow you to move freely.

Appropriate Footwear:

Wear shoes suitable for the playing surface, typically a hard or gravel surface. Comfortable sports shoes with non-slip soles are generally recommended.

No Bulky Jewelry:

Avoid wearing bulky or sharp jewelry that could cause injury to yourself or other players during throws.

Sun Protection:

If playing outdoors in sunny weather, it is wise to wear

a cap, sunglasses, and apply sunscreen to protect yourself from UV rays.

Personal Comfort:

Ensure you feel comfortable in your attire, as pétanque is a game that requires concentration and precision.

Team Jerseys:

In some cases, especially during team competitions or leagues, it is common for team members to wear matching jerseys with the team name.

Respect Local Rules:

Local competitions or specific tournaments may have their own rules or recommendations regarding attire. It is advisable to check the specific guidelines for the event you are participating in.

Overall, the key is to adhere to sportsmanship, demonstrate fair play, and ensure that your attire does not hinder your game or that of others. Keep in mind that pétanque is a friendly game where the pleasure of playing together takes precedence over the dress code.

Expressions in Pétanque and Their Meanings

Éric Borowiak, Journey to the Heart of Pétanque

Expressions in Pétanque

and Their Meanings

Games, whether they are board games, video games, sports, or others, often have specific expressions associated with their practice. These expressions result from a combination of tradition, effective communication, team spirit, strategy and tactics, and linguistic heritage. Over time, players develop a specific language unique to their game, which often becomes a tradition and an important cultural element.

These expressions facilitate communication between players, allowing them to quickly convey complex ideas or strategies during the game. Additionally, they reinforce the sense of belonging to a team or community and can have significant strategic or tactical meanings. Finally, these expressions can also reflect the linguistic or cultural history of the region where the game is played, thereby enriching the language associated with the game. The same is true for pétanque.

The Term "Mène"
in Pétanque

Éric Borowiak, Journey to the Heart of Pétanque

The Term "Mène"

in Pétanque

In pétanque, a "mène" is a round or a period of play during which teams compete to score points. A pétanque game is typically divided into several mènes, and the main objective of each mène is to place your boules as close as possible to the jack (cochonnet) while preventing the opposing team from doing the same.

Here is how a typical mène in pétanque unfolds:

One team starts by placing the jack at a determined distance on the playing field. The jack serves as the target that players must aim for with their boules.

Players from each team then take turns throwing their boules, aiming to place them as close as possible to the jack. Players can also shoot the opponent's boules to move them away from the jack.

At the end of the mène, points are awarded based on the proximity of the boules to the jack. The team with the boule closest to the jack scores one point, and each additional boule of the same team that is closer than the best boule of the opposing team scores an additional point. The team that scores the most points in a mène wins that mène.

The game continues with a new mène, where teams again choose strategies to place their boules advantageously.

A pétanque game can consist of a fixed number of mènes, such as 13 or 15, or it can be played until a team reaches a predefined number of points to win the game. Each mène offers players the opportunity to implement tactics and strategies to score points and ultimately win the game.

"Standing Feet Together"

Éric Borowiak, Journey to the Heart of Pétanque

"Se Tenir Pieds

Tanqués"

The expression "se tenir pieds tanqués" (Remain still with your feet firmly planted on the ground when throwing the ball) in pétanque refers to the player's position while playing. In pétanque, players throw their boules while standing still, unlike other boule games where movement is allowed.

"Se tenir pieds tanqués" means that players remain firmly anchored to the ground, with their feet well-positioned in relation to the jack (the small ball or target) and the boules already thrown. Proper foot positioning is important to ensure maximum stability during the throw and to maintain adequate balance during the game. This contributes to better precision and effectiveness in the game of pétanque.

"Kissing Fanny"

Éric Borowiak, Journey to the Heart of Pétanque

"Kissing Fanny"

The expression "Kissing Fanny" is used in the context of a game of boules when the final score reaches 13 to 0. In this situation, the losing player or team is traditionally required to kiss the bare bottom of a feminine representation known as Fanny.

According to a recent tradition, the origin of this practice dates back to a certain Fanny, a waitress in a café in Grand-Lemps shortly before World War I. The legend says that she allowed players who lost without scoring a single point to kiss her cheek as a consolation.

However, it is said that one day, a village magistrate, after losing, came to claim his reward. The popular version of the story suggests that Fanny, perhaps harboring a grudge against the magistrate, decided to humiliate him by lifting her skirt and offering him her buttock. Unfazed, the magistrate accepted, and two resounding kisses echoed in the café, thus inaugurating a tradition that endures.

However, since players cannot always rely on the presence of a real Fanny ready to reveal her buttock in public, a place of honor is reserved for the "fake Fanny" in all places where boules are played. The unfortunate losers are then forced, in front of an amused audience, to kiss the always plump buttock of a Fanny represented in a painting, sculpture, or in terracotta.

Thus, what was originally a reward has become the ultimate act of humiliation for any boules player.

""are you shooting or pointing ?"

Éric Borowiak, Journey to the Heart of Pétanque

"Are you shooting

or pointing?"

The familiar expression "Oh, are you shooting or pointing?" originates from the context of pétanque, a popular boules game. This phrase is often used humorously to tease a player when they have to decide on the strategy to adopt during their turn. It likely arose from the relaxed and convivial atmosphere that often surrounds pétanque games.

In pétanque, players face two main choices:

Shooting:

Involves throwing the boule with enough force to displace or eliminate the opponent's boules.

Pointing:

Involves gently placing the boule as close as possible to the jack without touching the other boules.

When someone asks, "Are you shooting or pointing?", they are referring to these two possible actions, highlighting the tactical dilemma the player faces. This expression has become a playful and friendly way to joke among pétanque players, illustrating the strategic and decision-making aspects of the game.

The expression has become emblematic of pétanque and is often used humorously during games. It reflects the social and interactive nature of this popular sport. Other expressions related to pétanque are often cited more or less frequently, adding to the unique charm of the game.

"Breaking Away"

Éric Borowiak Voyage au cœur de la pétanque

"Breaking

Away"

The expression "Breaking Away" in the game of boules, particularly in pétanque, is a familiar expression used to describe a situation where a boule leaves the playing field. In other words, the boule rolls or is shot out of the marked playing area, meaning it no longer has any influence on the course of the game.

The use of the expression "Breaking Away" is often tinged with a humorous or friendly tone, as it poetically or amusingly describes the boule leaving the field. It is a relaxed way of talking about a boule that has been eliminated from the game, whether intentionally by a shot or accidentally by a bad maneuver.

"You have to
pull hard"

Éric Borowiak, Journey to the Heart of Pétanque

"You have to

pull hard"

The expression "you need to shoot hard" in the game of boules, particularly in pétanque, means that it is necessary to make a shot or throw with more force, usually to dislodge one or more opponent's boules that are well positioned in relation to the jack.

"Shoot hard" refers to the weight of the lead (which was used in the making of pétanque boules), indicating that the boule should be thrown with enough force to strategically move the opponent's boules.

Thus, when someone says you need to "shoot hard," it suggests that the player must make a more powerful shot to change the arrangement of the boules on the field and improve their position in the game.

Dedication

"I warmly dedicate this book to Cathy and Pierre, whose welcoming, kindness, and friendliness have illuminated my experience with their pétanque team. My gratitude also extends to all the pétanque players who join them during these gatherings, sharing our common passion for pétanque. Their conviviality has greatly enriched this experience, and it is with deep appreciation that I address this dedication to them."

Éric Borowiak

By the same author:

The Glossary of Merchandising and Retail Distribution

The Employee's Bible in Business

Understanding Labor Courts and Their New Procedures: How to Successfully Manage Your Case

The Glossary of Automotive Mechanics and Its Environment

The Glossary of Culinary Expressions

Move, Eat, Breathe, and Balance Your Weight

Journey to the Heart of Pétanque

ÉRIC BOROWIAK
presented

Journey to the
Heart of Pétanque

Its history, its types of play, its rules

The Art of Shooting, Pointing, and Winning!

Published by Pierre Semard Editions

Printed in Dunstable, United Kingdom